PICTURING AMERICA

THOMAS COLE
and the
BIRTH OF AMERICAN ART

HUDSON TALBOTT

NANCY PAULSEN BOOKS

Dedicated to the village of
Catskill, New York,
birthplace of American art

NANCY PAULSEN BOOKS
an imprint of Penguin Random House LLC
375 Hudson Street, New York, NY 10014

Copyright © 2018 by Hudson Talbott.

Library of Congress Cataloging-in-Publication Data
Names: Talbott, Hudson, author, illustrator.
Title: Picturing America : Thomas Cole and the birth of American art / Hudson Talbott.
Description: New York : Nancy Paulsen Books, 2018. | Audience: Ages 6–8.
Identifiers: LCCN 2017060153 | ISBN 9780399548673 (hardback) | ISBN 9780399548703 (ebook) | ISBN 9780399548680 (ebook)
Subjects: LCSH: Cole, Thomas, 1801–1848—Juvenile literature. | Painters—United States—Biography—Juvenile literature. | Hudson River school of landscape
painting—Juvenile literature. | BISAC: JUVENILE NONFICTION / Biography & Autobiography / Art. | JUVENILE NONFICTION / Science & Nature /
General (see also headings under Animals or Technology). | JUVENILE NONFICTION / History / United States / 19th Century.
Classification: LCC ND237.C6 T35 2018 | DDC 759.13 [B]—dc23
LC record available at https://lccn.loc.gov/2017060153
Manufactured in China by RR Donnelley Asia Printing Solutions Ltd.
ISBN 9780399548673

1   3   5   7   9   10   8   6   4   2

Design by Eileen Savage. Text set in Vendetta.
Conceptual Design by Hudson Talbott.
The art was done in watercolors, colored pencil, and ink on Arches watercolor paper.

THOMAS COLE was a curious boy. He was always looking for
something new to draw. He and his sister Sarah took their sketchbooks
whenever they went out wandering in the English countryside. The
hedgerows were a good place to find something—a gnarly tree, a bug, or
perhaps a hedgehog, if they were lucky.

3

The landscape of their homeland had become a patchwork of farms and fields, dotted with villages like their own, Bolton. Thomas and Sarah usually had to search far for something they hadn't already drawn.

What truly sparked Thomas's imagination were the stories he heard of America and its vast wilderness. He dreamed of going there, even though his sisters laughed at the idea. But Thomas's dreams of America burned brighter as he watched England change.

The change that came to England was called the Industrial Revolution. It brought hard times to the Cole family, for machines were now taking the place of humans. Thomas's father had to close his workshop because he could not make goods as cheaply as the big factories. The family decided it was time to seek their fortune in America. Thomas's dream was coming true!

They arrived in Philadelphia in the
summer of 1818, after a four-week voyage.
Only three of Thomas's seven sisters
came along.

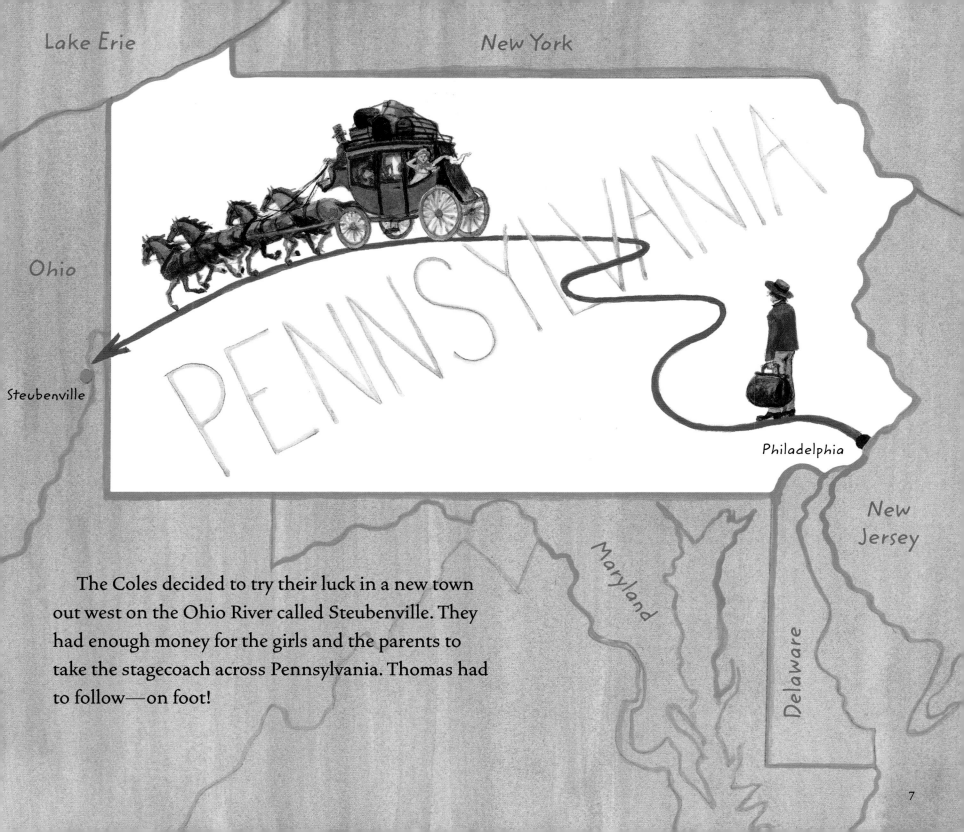

Lake Erie

New York

Ohio

PENNSYLVANIA

Steubenville

Philadelphia

New Jersey

Maryland

Delaware

The Coles decided to try their luck in a new town out west on the Ohio River called Steubenville. They had enough money for the girls and the parents to take the stagecoach across Pennsylvania. Thomas had to follow—on foot!

7

hand-painted window shades

In Steubenville, the Coles made lots of high-quality items. But it seemed that the town just wasn't ready for them. They tried many things to make ends meet, but life for the immigrant family was a struggle.

Meanwhile, Thomas's artistic skills kept improving. All his years of drawing were now helping him with his decorative designs. He drew every day, always pushing himself to do better. Then one day he got a lucky break. A traveling portrait painter came through Steubenville and befriended him.

hand-blocked wallpaper

hand-painted floor cloths

He showed Thomas how to blend oil paints on canvas. Then he lent the boy a book of fine art.

Thomas's mind exploded!

He had never seen art like that before! Suddenly Thomas knew what he wanted to do with his life.

So began Thomas Cole's journey to becoming an artist. He followed the example of the traveling artist and walked to neighboring towns, looking for painting jobs. But he had no luck. After weeks of tramping around the countryside, Thomas returned to Steubenville with only a dollar in his pocket. Worse, he found his family had moved again. Thomas followed them to Pittsburgh to help them start a new business.

But Thomas felt he needed to make his future in a place where people would pay for art. Even if it meant walking. For the second time, Thomas walked across Pennsylvania, this time with his art supplies strapped on his back and a tablecloth for an overcoat!

In Philadelphia he found work painting vases. It didn't last long.

Pittsburgh

Philadelphia

Winter in Philadelphia was hard. Thomas was tired and lonely but kept his dream alive by drawing constantly. Sometimes the guards at the art academy let him draw there at night. His spirits were lifted when he got word that his family had moved again—this time to New York City!

The only room he could afford had no bed and no heat. He lived on bread and water.

New York was the center of art and culture in America and Thomas was happy to be there, even if it was just in an attic above his family. He now had a place to make his paintings and to show them to potential customers. Among his visitors was a merchant named Thomas Bruen, who liked Thomas's landscapes. He suggested that the young artist take the steamer up the Hudson River to see the real American wilderness. He even offered to pay for the ticket. Thomas had his first patron!

The trip up the Hudson was a voyage of discovery for Thomas. As he passed the wild mountain ranges and vast forests along the river's edge he realized why he was on this journey. He was going there to paint America. He felt he had something to say and he was on his way to find it.

When the boat docked at Catskill Village, the passengers rushed out into waiting coaches. They were all headed up the mountain to a new resort called the Catskill Mountain House. They were there to escape the heat of the city and to enjoy a new American invention called a "vacation." Thomas didn't care where he slept. He was there to draw.

All summer long Thomas wandered with his sketchbook from dawn to dusk, often sleeping under the stars.

When autumn came, Thomas returned to the city. New paintings were soon
crowding him out of his studio. Thomas convinced a friendly bookstore owner
to put three of Thomas's pictures in his shop's window. One day, a famous artist
named John Trumbull saw them. He ran and told his friends, "I've discovered a
genius! It's what we've been looking for—a style of art that is 100% American!
Somebody named Cole has done it! Pure American landscapes—portraits of
our country!" He sat down to catch his breath and said quietly, "This youth has
done what I cannot do after fifty years' practice." *

The friends bought Thomas's paintings and added them to a major ex-
hibition at the American Academy. The work caused a sensation. Thomas was
invited to put his work in more shows and people began talking about him.

The CLOVE
by Thos. Cole

People were astounded at the dramatic natural beauty that Thomas captured on canvas. For city dwellers, nature had often been viewed fearfully from a distance. Now it was being celebrated.

Thomas's view of America struck a chord with the public. The young nation was still a little unsure of itself, but Thomas's landscapes gave people pride in their beautiful land. He soon became the toast of New York!

Despite his success, Thomas felt there was lots more to learn, and there was only one place to learn it—Europe.

LONDON

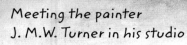
Meeting the painter
J. M.W. Turner in his studio

The boat to France

PARIS

Thomas's Travels in EUROPE

Thomas stayed for three years in Europe, soaking up its art and culture. In London, he met the great English landscape painters. His work was shown in exhibitions, but he was disappointed that the English didn't take it more seriously. After two lonely years he left for Paris. Then on to Italy.

FLORENCE

ROME

T. C. rented a room here.

Rome was the center of the art world in those days. Everyone who was anyone had to go there, including Thomas.

Thomas fell in love with Italy. The art, the history, the light, and the color all inspired him. The pasta was good too. In Florence he studied the art of the great masters. In Rome he sketched the ruins left by the ancient Roman Empire, and wondered how and why such a great power fell.

By the time he sailed for home Thomas was a changed man. His view of the world had grown far beyond his beloved Catskill Mountains. He had more to say.

POMPEII

21

When Thomas returned to the Catskills he became troubled by how much of the wild landscape had disappeared, just as it had in England. He feared that the industrialization of America would lead to its destruction. He wanted to send a warning. It had to be a statement that was powerful, even epic.

1

2

3

He came up with an idea for a series of paintings inspired by his time in Rome. He called it *The Course of Empire*. It included five scenes showing the rise and fall of a great empire: 1) its beginning in the wilderness; 2) living in harmony with nature; 3) becoming too powerful; 4) falling from power; 5) returning to wilderness. It shocked the public and made him the most famous artist in America.

Asher Durand — a close friend

Maria Cole — Thomas's wife

Frederic Church — a young student

The Cole's Family Home

CEDAR GROVE

Catskill, NY

The Cole children

Thomas returned every summer to the studio he rented on a farm near Catskill Village. It was there that he met and fell in love with the farmer's niece, Maria Bartow. They were soon married and moved into the main house, sharing it with her sisters, uncle, and many houseguests. Thomas's art students also joined him there to go sketching in the mountains. And soon, there were Cole children. It was a busy household.

Thomas loved the way the houses of ancient Rome were decorated, so
he gave his own walls a similar treatment. It was his way of sharing the
inspiration of Italy with everyone who came to his home. He never lost his
love for decorative painting, nor for Italy.

Thomas still loved to wander the hills with his sketch pad, but as the years passed, he used the time more for thinking. He looked back on his life and wondered if he had actually made a difference in the world. People often said that his art showed what it meant to be American. Now he simply wanted to show what it meant to be human.

To do that Thomas created a series of paintings portraying a person's journey through four stages of life. He called it *The Voyage of Life*, and it became his most famous work. Reproductions of it are still sold today.

Childhood
The first painting shows an innocent child in a golden boat at dawn, protected by a guardian angel.

Youth
By noontime the child is now a young man, leaving the angel behind as he goes out into the world to follow his dreams.

Thomas probably remembered his own journeys across Pennsylvania on foot, when his dreams kept him going.

Manhood

The man is now middle-aged, like Thomas. He is lost in a storm with a broken rudder. Alone in the world, he prays for help.

Old Age

It is now evening and the man is old and humbled by life's journey. His work is done. The angel has returned to guide him home.

Sadly, Thomas did not live to see this last phase of his own life. He died of a sudden illness six years after painting the series. America mourned his passing.

Thomas Cole left the world too soon, but his work launched a movement that became far more important than anything he could've imagined. His genius for capturing the American landscape drew other artists to follow him. Frederic Church, Asher Durand, and many others were inspired to paint natural scenery in a style that came to be known as the Hudson River school of art. It was the first art movement that was truly born in America.

But Thomas's influence went much further than art. Americans gradually came to understand his message of saving the environment while there was still time. By the 1870s large areas of pristine wilderness were being preserved from destruction. They eventually became our first national parks. This in turn led to the modern environmental movement, which continues to fight today to protect our forests, air, water and wildlife.

But the most important gift that Thomas Cole left us was his perspective on his beloved new country—the vision of a young artist for a young land full of promise and freedom. He showed us a way of picturing . . .

. . . America, the beautiful.

*The author wishes to express his thanks for the help
and support of the following people:*

BETSY JACKS, Executive Director,
Thomas Cole National Historic Site

DR. BETSY KORNHAUSER,
Curator of American Paintings and Sculpture,
Metropolitan Museum of Art

DR. ALAN WALLACH, Professor of Art and Art History,
The College of William and Mary

DR. NANCY SIEGEL,
Professor of Art History, Towson University

DR. TIM BARRINGER,
Professor of History of Art, Yale University